M000309332

A BLOOD CONDITION

BY THE SAME AUTHOR

Kumukanda

A BLOOD CONDITION

Kayo Chingonyi

Chatto & Windus
LONDON

1 3 5 7 9 10 8 6 4 2

Chatto & Windus, an imprint of Vintage,
is part of the Penguin Random House
group of companies whose addresses can be found at
global.penguinrandomhouse.com

Copyright © Kayo Chingonyi 2021

Kayo Chingonyi has asserted his right to be identified
as the author of this Work in accordance with the
Copyright, Designs and Patents Act 1988

First published in the UK by Chatto & Windus in 2021

penguin.co.uk/vintage

A CIP catalogue record for this book is available from the British Library

ISBN 9781784743901

Typeset in 11/14 pt Minion Pro
by Integra Software Services Pvt. Ltd, Pondicherry

Printed and bound in Great Britain by Clays Ltd, Elcograf S.p.A.

The authorised representative in the EEA is Penguin Random House Ireland,
Morrison Chambers, 32 Nassau Street, Dublin DO2 YH68.

Penguin Random House is committed to a sustainable future for
our business, our readers and our planet. This book is made from
Forest Stewardship Council® certified paper.

for Jasper & John

Contents

A BLOOD CONDITION

Nyaminyami

in a country named for its river, where the river is wide and its flow gives life to those who live on its banks, in a valley where people and the river lived in accord for generations, woven as hair in a braid is woven, in such a place our story begins, half a lifetime ago before the Monckton Commission when people burned their chitupas in front of the offices of district commissioners, before a blood condition passed through the populace as flame through forest, before load shedding, hours of power cuts; the national grid sold off to the highest bidder, before Zed was booming from copper, its roads full of American cars and salesmen plied their trade with sweet nothings, weaving through the traffic to make their entreaties: my friend you must hurry up and catch this Mustang before it gallops away. Before potholes and roads unfinished through lack of investment, before imported knock offs, before the goods trains and trucks, before the valley was connected by the orderly topography of macadam and the valley's foot-worn pathways, taught to the valley's young by experience, were paved. The valley people lived in a relative peace. Livingstone was, by then, long dead and the people were free to bide after their own fashion, giving honour to the god of the river and, in return for their supplication, receiving blessings in the form of fish so plentiful that to a child who did not like fish a parent would say my darling, here, there is fish or there is fish and the child would remember the legacy knitted in to the songs they had known all their lives of fisherfolk who swam before they could walk or talk because the river god would never let them sink

Nyaminyami: ...the river god

like many gods is a vengeful god   but who would not
want vengeance   separated from   their lover
by the insistence of machinery   the promise of copper
the future   open   to those brave enough to take it
always this human mania for taking   the river god
remembers   what is forgotten   between generations
slavers raided   in the name   of this self-same progress
and who was it   through all of this   who   provided
no man   nothing so inflexible as that   but this god
part serpent   though don't believe what they tell you
about serpents   part fish   able to swim   and be one
with water   holding water   in a flowing order
no man-made machine   could conjure   though the strangers
who came with their ideas   of order   their instruments
and blueprints   those strangers brought with them a plan
to build a dam   harness the river's power to bolster
the power of man   and what did it matter to them
dishonouring   a god   in whom they didn't believe

for those who believed   the dam   was no boon
they knew   no human hand could bend the landscape
to the ends of capital   without consequence
and so they offered prayers   and bade their kinfolk
agree to nothing   sign nothing   refuse the handshakes
that   to these strangers   constitute contracts
and though believers feared the river god's wrath
the dam was built   the strangers executed their plan
and what did it matter that the skies brought forth
unprecedented rain   a mere trifle   and those swept away

were unlucky but what had that to do with the dam
which would bring about such prosperity in this land
believers knew   the waters raged   in the river god's name
that in the quest for progress   we often make mistakes
make beds   in which our descendants sleep badly
in our haste to acquire to own to feed
a monster which cannot be sated   for all you fill
with minerals its   waiting   capacious   mouth

Origin Myth

Zero

1920, nine years before Nellie
is born, a ghost note in simian blood
is loosed by a novice butcher's unsteady
knife-work. Rubies scattering in the mud.
Making a fist she raises it up
to stem the flow and marvel as it slows;
a haemoglobin beck under her toes.

A decade or more before the penny
drops; this blood-punter already abroad
(the names of the dead will always be heavy
as a colony of ants drinking from a gourd).
Men who love men sup on the freedom to love
each other; step together out of clothes
after dancing in clubs that never close.

Miguel

After dancing in clubs that never close
his allegiance is to a Hammond B3
that, if you play it right, will disclose,
by sympathetic magic of its stuck key,
the traces of a blacker melody.

After church he plays the devil's music,
fingers tap a boogie-speckled blues riff
in praise of fingertips brushing a nose,
deliberate, a darkened corner's hungry
trysts, hips scoring the music's crescendos.

Accustomed to underlay, the seedy
sides of town, he favours bars whose heady
mix of high and low he finds therapeutic
(acquaintance with the night has its uses).

Erykah

Acquaintance with the night has its uses
in life given over to capital,
its envoys, the trade-offs it produces.
All we build to sublimate animal
selves. She knows this like she knows this hospital –
bedpan by soiled bedpan. Where she meets Miguel

here to see a friend from forty deuces's
alternate marketplace; call him Confucius.
Mid-smoke he tests his latest philosophical
premise, claims freewill is impossible,
every confidence trickster has a tell;
the nucleus of an infected cell.

Viral

The nucleus of an infected cell
is a pathogen's ultimate gateway –
after the breach, the sounding of a knell,
the ending of a life, or so they say.
I believed it, too, to my great shame,
as did my mother who refused the pills
that would have her here among us still.

The lobby of a Shoreditch hotel,
Miguel is now our aging DJ
holding the headphone to his ear like a shell
living after so much death. A cliché
of his times that taught him to live day to day.
The dancers heave and swell, in search of thrills,
like droplets moistening a windowsill.

Results

Like droplets moistening a windowsill
is how you might, if you were so inclined,
describe nervous energy's overspill
into panic. Waiting for the call, you find
monolithic tombstones occupy your mind;
recalling ads from the decade of Thatcher
that passed judgement and prophesied rapture.

All clear. Sat in bed you cry until
streetlights glance the lattice of the blinds,
your heart a boulder rolling down a hill
your optimism toughened to a rind
effective, if a little unrefined.
And though, for now, you're spared the hereafter
there are depths of fear no words can capture.

Survivor's Guilt

There are depths of fear no words can capture.
What to do, having been granted reprieve,
with what remains of your life? What if, after
the storm has passed the pasture is relieved
of its fertility? And who to thank for all that you achieve,
given time to work on your vocation,
what spectres attend the celebration?

For all the outward signs you manufacture
pointing to wellness, the stages you complete,
running through the middle there's this fracture.
Each living moment carries a receipt –
as doubting is the price of your belief.
May god bless this blood-borne innovation
sired somewhere in the Congo Basin.

Origin Myth

Sired somewhere in the Congo basin
yet how it grew to populate the earth
teaching us the story of mutation
is the story that attends the very birth
of our kind, the tenuous nature of our worth.
Is it any wonder the road seems so unsteady?
Millions lost to veering paths already.

For those who came before me, a libation!
I conjure you as though we sat around a hearth
when I walk it's your shadow I'm chasing.
Next to my skin I still carry the hurt
finely woven as a cambric shirt
from before akashishi* took so many:
1920, nine years before Nellie.

---

* The Bemba phrase 'Bamalwele ya akashishi' means
'Those who suffer from the germ/virus'.

Forgive

Green-eyed boy,
I write this from where you left off   *the land of the living*   so called.

And how do you like your digs are you somewhere now bumping dark riddims
cut with a thread of light?

What a time to be alive *everyone's going on spare not just my life going on pear*
have I told you about this recurring nightmare:

a hammer   coming down on a tree stump my hand   waiting on the stump for the blow?

I learned of your passing as I dressed for a wedding
shifting the knot of my tie I said *ok* – marvelling

at the way a stock phrase insinuates itself the way certain man spread
to fill a space –

we hadn't spoken in months   had I known the words *bruv, what is good*
would be the last words

of our correspondence I would have told you how the table and chairs in your
mother's kitchen rebuilt me.

I would have asked if you remembered the day we heard krystal klear on rinse and
glimpsed joy long enough to dance.

Blues for Albert 'Prodigy' Johnson & Carl 'Haystee' Samuel

Another scribe of black trauma has passed
from this life into the spirit world
or nothingness depending on how much
store you set by Nietzsche –
apt that the arch-laureate of nihilism
comes to mind when I think
of Prodigy, old before his time,
as I was old before mine.

*

We passed a zoot
rolled with torcedor finesse
round a circle in Barking
(before it had a health spa).

One of our number was confined,
these times, to his room by shame,
a death of some kind,

because, lying under a sky
pockmarked with stars, he asked
his girlfriend why she was so quiet.

*

When Haystee walked
or fell in front of the lorry
did he *pass away*
if I can still hear him
going back to back

with Kaystar and Rapsz
if I think of him
standing shoulder to shoulder
with Prodigy, in a circle
of dead emcees,
screwing up his face
singing:

> Listen up, I'm so raw-ah
> you know I'm MC Haystee
> and I'm on tour-ah
> when I spit my lyrics
> dem a shout more-ah
> and when I give you more
> the people dem will be so sore-ah?

*

In the year of our lord
two double oh three
Toks was still passing
himself off
as *Little Dizzee*
though Toks
was by then
closer in height to Jamakabi.

After *Lord of the Mics* dropped
the gas was such
it just took a younger

bussin' a half-decent
beatbox for the clash
to start. Everyone played
their part – from the hype-
men spitting lines back

like a space echo
to those standing
outside the cypher
but close enough
to cuss the vanquished
when a gap opened for him
to walk in the unforgiving
light of mediocrity.

This was before anyone
in our circle had been
stabbed or shifted.
Some had shouldered
a wooden box
but none of us understood
the cost of the shanks
and skengs in our lyrics.

If we knew those days as halcyon
is hard to say.
The mind is some next ends;
we wouldn't have been caught dead
slipping – convinced
as we were the patch of grass
beside *The Golden Fish*
was big enough to constitute a world.

16 Bars for the Bits

The old men who meet at the same time each evening
the youngers get bladdered and stagger; the heaving
the chatter of pigeons emboldened while feeding
and towers that balance at heights beyond reason
a beacon for dreamers and schemers and heathens
you can find angels behaving like demons
in ends where the rents seem to change with the seasons
and murder rates rise when the temperature's peaking
friends changing tack interrupted while speaking
students in packs only back for the weekend
the steadfast who waited and think about leaving
the homeless in parks making bargains with breathing
the lights in the dark guide you home and you're sleeping
or tossing and turning or scratching and wheezing
or thinking all night through the secrets you're keeping
and all this can come in the space of an evening.

a northerly aspect

we flew south –
and, though
wandsworth
alleyways
banished howays
from my diction,
still my heart
has a northerly aspect

(quite apart
from this voice
that divides opinion
when I carry it
far from home).

How to gesture
towards tall ships
grace darling
bottles of pop
bobby shafto
the part of me
lost to the realm
of ledgers
of legend

the part
that ascribes
to darkness
light
here where the landscape

is a long conversation
and the breeze
a list of the missing
and of the dead
read from the surface
of these stones
that do not forget.

Guy's and St Thomas's

When I'm here in a particular
character of mind
any woman of a certain height –
hair plaited neat
to meet the working day –
becomes my mother
in that year of early mornings
she worked at GDRU
close to this stretch of the river
close to Hay's Galleria;
the aquarium that is still here
though she is not
to walk with me as we scrutinize
tropical fish
laughing in the uncomplicated
manner that comes
of understanding. And after,
a bankside stroll

a cart-proprietor advertises wares;
varieties of ice cream.
It is 1999. My last summer as native
this side of the river
where the water brings pilgrims in search
of a cure for long hours,
bad coffee, friends
always catching up
and rarely giving conversation its due.
How can I set down
the passage of time? Who knew a face

becomes less and less distinct
the longer it no longer exists?
How to lift this mist
from my eyes, that I might see
this concrete and glass
for what it is and stop
writing my mother into it
that I might let her walk away
becoming smaller and smaller
until she disappears.

13 Napier Street

The latch
capitulates
step-dad
doesn't whistle
walks through
the cream door
hunched
plucks
the remote
from the coffee table
mutes
Scooby Do
on the Grundig.

Longing

Towards   the end
when she   drifted   beyond the reach
of human medicine   my mother
assembled a necklace of denominations.

Pentecostal   Roman Catholic
Seventh Day Adventist   Anglican
and the African Church   that met in a school
of which   my mother   myself   and the pastor
were   the entire congregation.

From   this six-month   I remember best
a Christian Science Reading Room
in Richmond   mum leafing through
a copy   of *The Monitor*
placing   her faith
in words   lifted to the frequency

of longing   a pitch so lofty
only a celestial ear   could bend to it
and   if the ear belonged to [a] person[s]
outside time   that being   those beings
might grant divine providence;
                    give my mother a sign.

Ginnel

1.

an interstice
        a quarter-tone
last known
whereabouts
of missing persons
the world over

2.

From the Old English:
the coast's open maw
pointing the way
to the whale road

3.

gap in the teeth
of a terraced street

Love

1.

hang around
this town
will mind you
of how little
you need

2.

to speak
and find an echo
breathe
good air
amid
mid-afternoon's
demands

3.

as a water droplet
falls from spring leaves
indiscriminate endearment
fleck of grace
it lands
I see you

Loppy

1.

As *threat* is to *vengeful mass*
so this epithet stands-
in for striplings
who, like the colliers,
and mill workers,
and smiths
before them,
kept the wolf from the door
in the muck
beating a steady rhythm
from the argument
of sweat and ore

2.

dust-begrimed
soap-skeptic
dutty
dusty
crusty

3.

a thing on which to build
if you can see past the surface
a waistcoat of filth
uniform of an ancient guild

Arguments in favour of the sea

1. Dayclean

2. Cold day, one week after we wed,
    the woman I love
    inching in to swim

3. Water passing over stones
    sounds like my auntie weaving family
    history as if she sat at a loom

4. Four years ago
    with a man I look like
    who looks like me
    rental bikes
    shoreline promenade
    denim shirt
    billowing
    the presence of mind
    to take a picture.

5. Chastising wind
    knuckles raw
    in that first Newcastle
    winter

6. Turning to watch the mist
    clip the top of Table Mountain
    two years out of university
    with no job

but this wandering
to speak in far-off rooms.

7.   Waterlogged shore road
to Kilcreggan, tugboats
performing their routine

8.   The switch up 3 minutes 30 into 'Nights'
that October
everything turned
in such small moments
proposals of marriage
had become our running joke.
That day we returned
to the operative words.

9.   The tall ships
Their figures so prominent
in remembrance
it doesn't matter
whether I saw them or not

10.   Swing seat
in front of a shop selling
gelato and agua frescas
toes brushing sand

11. Long subway ride
     pensioners
     trying to slow down time.
     At some distance
     screams from a hundred-
     year-old roller coaster.

12. Sea spray

Chingola Road Cemetery

Because of what it would take to visit
I visit tata's grave on Street View
in the early hours of mornings when
the edge of sleep is like the border at Kasumbalesa

where men with red eyes
police their sovereign patch,
Kalashnikovs at their sides;
gold standard of summary justice,
making, of a family, cartographers then sextons.

Our year nine biology teacher glossed succession:
the built environment
will always be exposed as a fad, given time.
And so, it has come to pass here
the Chingonyi name's resting place.

This is a picture of David (late),
and Muzanga (equally late),
and John Kanjamba (also late),

where we might find a stone
it is overgrown with long grasses
and plants designated weeds
because we've yet to lend them use.

I came to pay my respects
As did my mother before me
kneeling at the exact spot
all she carried, like a bag of shopping,
dropped; its contents rolling.

On the tape she made
of his favourite songs
her voice cracks
in the act of speaking
as if the act is what loosed him
from this plane.

Let us pause to play him 'Hotel California'
let us say father and son
are driving together
along a coastal road
in an open top feat
of mid-century automotive nous

the son rides shotgun
skipping tunes to test
the low end of the Altec Lansing
system in the back
as one track fades
another picks up the slack

a wayfarer's tune
written in a shack
on a four track
in the 70s:
guitar
a voice threaded with regret
each word a promise
that in the end
the singer could not keep.

Postcard from the Sholebrokes

For Tony Harrison

Ciroc bottles and nitrous canisters
far cry from dance floors and night club bannisters
the youngers sing *blessings on blessings on blessings*
pouring a sip for departed bredrins
lost to the brief imposition of blades;
or jailhouse; or another city's grey
skyline, better because of its distance;
hitting the books; or freestyling fictions
to big up their chests. They ride for their ends
on quad bikes and pushbikes this circle of friends.

In this corner of your corner of the world,
Tony, that scrap of contested land curled
in your books, facing the street's chiaroscuro
I look on, lost in this writing bureau
fifty-year emblem from Sutcliffe & Son;
late thread in the fabric of Todmorden.

landscape w/ motorway

tessellated lives   unfolding
as   a flurry of words   unfolds
in an underpass cypher   and ciphers
   scrawled on brickwork

the wind   spits the sickest bars
both   about and through   this landscape
no less worthy of our gaze   for being
made   as a ceramic receptacle   for meaning   is made

and a link   between   concepts
and   *all that is the case*   is made
and Wittgenstein's thesis   and our means
of apprehending it   crafted by some hand

here   the spot a car abandoned its original
trajectory   here   a squabble turned final
here   a wayside shrine   a warning sign
a monument unmarked for all but those

who hold   this place   suspended
in the mind   who walk   in the ruins
of a bygone   ends   that exists
in the tense of potential   but nonetheless   exists

The last night of my 20s

For Roddy Lumsden

Fitting that the day should dawn
in this most Lumsdenesque of Lumsdenesque
contexts: sea-froth for night music
and the company of Suzannah –
kind enough to show me this walk
she knows without recourse to light.

When the hour came
'Mr Brightside' played it in
a song to which
      by dint of the glint
          in Sophie Barnard's eye
               twelve years ago
I cannot listen passively.

Which calls to mind the secret canticle
that undoes you, Roderick.
Maybe it is better some things
retain their mist
that all of us might carry a well of myth
in the pit of our pith,
maybe it is by such melodies we exist.

Heirlooms

The stein
with a
chipped edge
you're sure
you bought
for a
quid
in Camden
belonged,
if you
ask me
as well
you might
to my
mother,
known
all her life
by
a name
she detested.

What does
it mean
to answer
to a
misnomer;
to feel
the cold
air between
being and
being seen?

We have
filled
our house
with her
things:
Alfred Meakin
dinner set,
cutlery etched
with the
indicia
of the
Newcastle Corporation;
made in
Sheffield
by Firth Steelworks,
a white drop leaf,
crystalline glassware,
a house-proud
woman's cache.

I live
in an
artist's impression
of the
flat in
Wandsworth.
I cut
vegetables
with the
knife

my mother
reached for
in rage.
I remember
the sound
of metal
scraping wood;
the door
I had
just grown
strong enough
to hold
closed.

Genealogy

[Chilufya Nellie]

Grandfather, on visiting the village,
found there a woman in the throes of pregnancy
with whom he struck a bargain:
if he is a boy, I will be his friend
and if you birth a girl, I will marry her.
This girl became your mother.

[Chilufya Jasper]

There you are, Ba Jasper, in the flat on Cavendish Place
sat beside the cloth you inherited from my grandmother,
of which I still have a tattered strip.
The fullness in your cheeks puts you pre-diagnosis.
How remiss of me to have forgotten the quality of your smile.

[Umwana]

What do we mean when we say we see, in the face
of an infant, this or that characteristic?
Who am I to recognize, here, in what I know is a portrait
from a time that cannot, any longer, be?

[Shieldfield]

They let you hold them before taking them away.
You were enraptured by their bow-leggedness,
those legs that never ran down these stairs and along the road.
I always say: *I was supposed to have three siblings.*

[Inheritance]

Amid the clothes and shoes and electronics,
this, your most apposite bequest: a box of cassettes,
each one signed with your initials,
that we might once again inhabit the same room.

[Express Mail]

To say something of equatorial sky:
what the mind cannot remember
the body knows. So it is I still feel the breeze
tickling the hairs on my arms.

[Hyem]

What became of canny and cannae and divvint?
Words, sharp as dandelion and burdock on the tongue,
lost to me as those I left at the gates
of the fee-paying school in Mufulira
where I was mocked for my demotic bemba.

[Malaika Chilufya]

Above almost anything, your namesake
likes to sit at your graveside.
To think our fear of these resting places
might be learned.

[No Ball Games]

1995. Stephen Lawrence two years gone.
This country's elementary lesson
in harm taught me to fight;
that following rules didn't mean I would survive.

[Family Portrait]

And if every image is
a self-portrait of the photographer
I praise what stirred in whoever is behind the camera
to take this picture of my mother and me at my father's grave.

[Long Joe]

The years bring out Tata's likeness.
When I visit his brother, who never thought
he would see me again in this life,
he says, in my dark glasses, I look just like him.

[Incantation]

The woman I came to your grave
to tell you about
wore your wedding ring
the day we married. And if, as I sometimes believe,
objects transmit energy,
this wearing brought you back.

[Clearance]

Your worldly possessions are gathering dust
in a storage unit off Goodmayes High Road.
No one will take the dressing table.
What need have we for these ornaments,
old textbooks, the wedding dress you never wore?

[Y2K]

The year clouded with news of a virus
that will decimate all digital life
passes like any year except
it leaves you behind
two months after my thirteenth birthday.

[Woodchip Effect]

Why, even now, it is preferable the person
speaking would just come out with it
goes back to an afternoon I was nineteen
waiting for the call; my test results.
I had it in my head that it would be bad news.

[Cream of Tomato Soup]

Mother's nakedness –
how bony she was –
she asked me not to be ashamed,
since I was cut from the place I wouldn't look.

[Epiphany]

I've lost a sharp recollection of her face
as it was when she lived
the face we take with us to our long homes
the face that is our last and only face
hiding under the subterfuge of flesh.

[Living Memory]

At the congress of orphans
we start proceedings
by welcoming those new to the fold.
And, does it get easier?
It doesn't get easier.

[A Cambric Shirt]

Canticle from childhood.
A song that teaches better, maybe,
than any song
the impossibility of keeping those we love.

[Conference Call]

A few days before the day
we commemorate the day
you were laid to rest
we reminisce, bring you back to dwell in our midst.

Epithalamium

there should be a poem
to bless the hands
that   cut   and salted
a bag of limes
the hands that brought
that bag aboard this boat
across a body of water
we can touch but cannot see

a poem of praise should
issue forth from the ether
in celebration of an island's
night-time fevers   secular benedictions
shot after   shot
we drink to the universal language
of wavy   turned up   smashed
passing Cuervo between us

and tentative questions
in all we have of each other's
words   me with a mouthful
of stock phrases   you fluent
almost   in this dancing tongue
our fellow passengers know
like they know the proper
way to nice up a journey home

after the dance
when the light has faded
and the music resounds
from a point beyond
the horizon   and this boat
we boarded guides us
gentle as a hand on a back
to the rest of our lives

interior w/ ceiling fan

wish that we could lie here
for the rest of our lives
the blades of the fan above us
whirling like a tanguera's skirt
everything outside this room
a distant country
let me be this unguarded always
speaking without need of words
because breath is the oldest language
any of us know

Nyaminyami: 'water can crash and water can flow'

who gave them   licence   to live   here
who brought them   succour   refuge
what gave them   the right
to come between   this centuries-old   love
what do they know   of love
who have not loved   outside   human time
this wall they built   in all their wisdom
can only delay   our union
those   who know water   know
eventually water will pass through
even   the smallest gap   in what appears
to the human eye   to be   a solid mass

Nyaminyami: epilogue

it is said that after the concrete
after the rain
after the valley
shifted from its old ways
all that remained
of nyaminyami
was a small statue
marking the place

a fish-headed snake
a caption
consigning the river god
to fable
as if all this water
flowed here by some accident
as if the old ways
were only stories

but to this day pilgrims
sometimes see a momentary swell
in the course of the river
and those who recognize these eddies
know this to be nyaminyami testing
the limits of human ingenuity
calling out to a lover who is constant
as the motion of water

Acknowledgements

Many thanks to the following who first commissioned or published some of these poems, or versions of them: Bedtime Stories for The End of The World Podcast; *Ink Tales: Bedtime Stories for the End of the World* (Bonnier, 2020); *Too Young, Too Loud, Too Different* (Corsair, 2021); The Adrian Brinkerhoff Foundation; Poet In The City; Durham Book Festival; Speaking Volumes; Sam Winston; Iain Chambers; Bethan Lloyd Worthington; *Poetry Ireland Review*; *New Statesman*; and *Granta*.

I would like, as always, to thank Parisa Ebrahimi whose sense of the internal structures of a poetry collection is illuminating, instructive, and inspirational. Thanks also to Clara Farmer, Charlotte Humphery, and Mia Quibell-Smith whose attention to detail, care, and passion have served my work exceptionally well.

I would also like to extend my gratitude to Chris Wellbelove, Monica MacSwan, and the whole Aitken Alexander team.

For the day ones and the new ones who have helped me through the difficult business of living. You know who you are. This book is a testament to your sacrifices, care, understanding and love.

Particular thanks to Sarah Perry for her incisive critique, boundless support, and love. Without you this book would not exist.

Thank you to all the families to which I belong but especially Auntie Florence, Uncle Ken, Kate, David, Kaimba, Sempela, Chilufya, Katai, Louise, Yande, Jake, Myriam, Ben, Leanne, Adina, Malaika, Naima, and Mylo.